Two Covenants

Dalen Garris
Revivalfire Ministries

This is a work of history. Historical individuals and places and events are mentioned.

Copyright © 2021 by Dalen Garris

Published by Revivalfire Ministries

ISBN 13:978-1-7342213-8-1

All rights reserved.
No part of this book may be used or reproduced in any manner whatsoever, without written permission, except in the case of brief quotations embodied in critical articles and reviews, as provided by U.S. Copyright Law.

Cover design by Kevin Haislip

For information, address
dale@revivalfire.org

First paperback printing June, 2021

Printed in the United States of America

Why seek ye the living among the dead?
(Luke 24:5)

Table of Contents

Forward	7
Compelling the Gentiles to live as the Jews	9
The Sabbath, Jewish holidays, and festivals	11
Dietary Laws	13
New Covenant vs. Old Covenant	17
About the Author	39
Publications	41

Forward

There is a doctrine emerging that contends that we must keep all the ordinances of the Old Law, including the feasts, dietary laws, Sabbaths, and even the blood sacrifices. It is an attempt to enhance the New Covenant with an adherence to the Torah. It has rightly been called a "Torah-based Faith".

I have noticed that God established His covenant with Abraham in Genesis 15 by passing through the parts of the sacrifice, the established way to confirm a covenant in the Old Testament (see Jeremiah 34:15). He established the New Covenant in the same way when Jesus Christ passed between the two parts (the thieves) and established His Covenant with mankind when He offered Himself as the only blood sacrifice that can really take away sin. There was no such thing done at Sinai.

I have no desire to argue with those who attempt to approach righteousness through carnal or legalistic means, other than to say that their doctrine is an attempt to nullify the Blood of Jesus, who died to set us free.

Rather than argue the point, I will let the Word of God speak for itself.

Compelling the Gentiles to live as the Jews

These are the dietary laws and the laws concerning the observance of the Sabbath, both which are major elements of the Law. If these are done away with, then so is the Law that is built upon them.

Acts 15: 19-20

Wherefore my sentence is, that we trouble not them, which from among the Gentiles are turned to God: But that we write unto them, that they abstain from pollutions of idols, and from fornication, and from things strangled, and from blood.

[Paul and Barnabas had no sooner come to Antioch on the heels of a wildly successful trip across Asia bringing the Gospel to the Gentiles, when Jewish Christians came down from Judea to tell them that the Gentiles had to be circumcised or they would burn in hell. The heated debate between them and the Apostles resulted in a minimal set of rules.

Nothing was said about keeping the Sabbath, dietary restrictions, or observing Jewish festivals. Besides that, nothing is mentioned about those requirements in all of Paul's epistles, across the entire New Testament, or any of the early church records.

If these Jewish restrictions are never mentioned, much less commanded anywhere in the New Testament, why is it so important to institute them now?]

Galatians 2:14-16

But when I saw that they walked not uprightly according to the truth of the gospel, I said unto Peter before them all, If thou, being a Jew, livest after the manner of Gentiles, and not as do the Jews, why compellest thou the Gentiles to live as do the Jews?

We who are Jews by nature, and not sinners of the Gentiles,

Knowing that a man is not justified by the works of the law, but by the faith of Jesus Christ, even we have believed in Jesus Christ, that we might be justified by the faith of Christ, and not by the works of the law: for by the works of the law shall no flesh be justified."

[There is no evidence that Gentile Christians worshipped on Saturday, ate only kosher foods, or observed Jewish feasts. We are not to allow anyone to try and bring us into bondage by saying that God's Word says otherwise.]

The Sabbath, Jewish holidays, and festivals

Colossians 2:16-17

Let no man therefore judge you in meat, or in drink, or in respect of an holyday, or of the new moon, or of the sabbath days: Which are a shadow of things to come; but the body is of Christ.

Romans 14:5

One man esteemeth one day above another: another esteemeth every day alike. Let every man be fully persuaded in his own mind.

John 9:16

Therefore said some of the Pharisees, This man is not of God, because he keepeth not the sabbath day. Others said, How can a man that is a sinner do such miracles? And there was a division among them.

Mark 2:27

And he said unto them, The sabbath was made for man, and not man for the sabbath:

Romans 14: 5,6

One man esteemeth one day above another: another esteemeth every day *alike*. Let every man be fully persuaded in his own mind.

He that regardeth the day, regardeth *it* unto the Lord; and he that regardeth not the day, to the Lord he doth not regard *it*.

Dietary Laws

Jesus declared all foods clean. The Levitical dietary restrictions are no longer in effect.

Mark 7:15

There is nothing from without a man, that entering into him can defile him: but the things which come out of him, those are they that defile the man.

Mark 7:18-20

And he saith unto them, Are ye so without understanding also? Do ye not perceive, that whatsoever thing from without entereth into the man, it cannot defile him;

Because it entereth not into his heart, but into the belly, and goeth out into the draught, purging all meats?

And he said, That which cometh out of the man, that defileth the man.

1 Timothy 4:3

Forbidding to marry, and commanding to abstain from meats, which God hath created to be received with thanksgiving of them which believe and know the truth.

1 Timothy 4:4-5

For every creature of God *is* good, and nothing to be refused, if it be received with thanksgiving:
For it is sanctified by the word of God and prayer.

Romans 14:6

He that eateth, eateth to the Lord, for he giveth God thanks; and he that eateth not, to the Lord he eateth not, and giveth God thanks.

Romans 14:14

I know, and am persuaded by the Lord Jesus, that *there is* nothing unclean of itself: but to him that esteemeth anything to be unclean, to him *it is* unclean.

Colossians 2:20-23

Wherefore if ye be dead with Christ from the rudiments of the world, why, as though living in the world, are ye subject to ordinances,
(Touch not; taste not; handle not;
Which all are to perish with the using;) after the commandments and doctrines of men?

Colossians 2:16

Let no man therefore judge you in meat, or in drink, or in respect of an holyday, or of the new moon, or of the sabbath *days:*

[Not only is there no restriction on which foods you can eat, it is commanded that you not criticize or judge someone else about that.]

Colossians 2:17

Which are a shadow of things to come; but the body *is* of Christ.

[The laws of the clean and unclean actually have little to do with your diet and more to do with separation from sin and worldliness.

A clean animal had two characteristics: it had cloven hooves and it had to chew the cud. It may be said that cloven hooves symbolize walking in righteousness by rightly dividing the way you walked, and chewing the cud symbolizes meditating and digesting the Bread of Life. Fish had to have scales, which could be seen as a protection from a sea of sin that surrounds us.

The sabbath of rest has many symbolic meanings, the most obvious would be resting from our works and allowing God to work through us. The 7th day had to do with the Old Covenant through Moses, while the 8th day, the Lord's Day, had to do with the new resurrection and new life through Jesus Christ]

1 Corinthians 8:8

But meat commendeth us not to God: for neither, if we eat, are we the better; neither, if we eat not, are we the worse.

Romans 14:17

For the kingdom of God is not meat and drink; but righteousness, and peace, and joy in the Holy Ghost.

New Covenant vs. Old Covenant

Acts 15:19-20

Wherefore my sentence is, that we trouble not them, which from among the Gentiles are turned to God: But that we write unto them, that they abstain from pollutions of idols, and from fornication, and from things strangled, and from blood.

Forasmuch as we have heard, that certain which went out from us have troubled you with words, <u>subverting your souls, saying, Ye must be circumcised, and keep the law</u>: to whom we gave no such commandment:

Matthew 11:13

For all the prophets and the law prophesied until John.

[If the Law ended at John's appearance, that would mean that a new covenant based on mercy and repentance rather than blood sacrifices was to be established.]

Luke 16:16

The law and the prophets were until John: since that time the kingdom of God is preached, and every man presseth into it.

[In other words, the Law is finished as we move into the covenant of Grace.]

John 4:21-24

Jesus saith unto her, Woman, believe me, the hour cometh, when ye shall neither in this mountain, nor yet at Jerusalem, worship the Father.

Ye worship ye know not what: we know what we worship: for salvation is of the Jews.

But the hour cometh, and now is, when the true worshippers shall worship the Father in spirit and in truth: for the Father seeketh such to worship him.

God is a Spirit: and they that worship him must worship him in spirit and in truth.

[It is time for a difference in worship, which indicates that the old way is no longer acceptable.]

Zechariah 11:10-12

And I took my staff, even Beauty, and cut it asunder, that I might break my covenant which I had made with all the people.

And it was broken in that day: and so the poor of the flock that waited upon me knew that it was the word of the LORD.

And I said unto them, If ye think good, give me my price; and if not, forbear. So they weighed for my price thirty pieces of silver.

[Jesus was that staff called Beauty and he was killed so that the Old Covenant could be broken for us so that we would no longer be under a covenant that could not deliver us from sin.]

Ezekiel 16:59-63

For thus saith the Lord GOD; I will even deal with thee as thou hast done, which hast despised the oath in breaking the covenant.

Nevertheless, I will remember my covenant with thee in the days of thy youth, and <u>I will establish unto thee an everlasting covenant</u>.

Then thou shalt remember thy ways, and be ashamed, when thou shalt receive thy sisters, thine elder and thy younger: and I will give them unto thee for daughters, <u>but not by thy covenant</u>.

And I will establish my covenant with thee; and thou shalt know that I am the LORD:

That thou mayest remember, and be confounded, and never open thy mouth anymore because of thy shame, when I am pacified toward thee for all that thou hast done, saith the Lord GOD.

[God is telling the Israelites that He will establish a new covenant with them because they broke the old one. But this new one will not be like "thy" covenant, in other words the one you already have, but this would be a new covenant.]

Jeremiah 31:31-33

Behold, the days come, saith the LORD, that I will make a new covenant with the house of Israel, and with the house of Judah:

Not according to the covenant that I made with their fathers in the day that I took them by the hand to bring them out of the land of Egypt; which my covenant they brake, although I was an husband unto them, saith the LORD:

But this shall be the covenant that I will make with the house of Israel; After those days, saith the LORD, I will put my law in their inward parts, and write it in their hearts; and will be their God, and they shall be my people.

[Again, God is telling them in advance that the old covenant is going to be replaced by a new one, making the old one no longer valid.]

Hebrews 8:6-13

But now hath he obtained a more excellent ministry, by how much also he is the mediator of a <u>better covenant</u>, which was established upon better promises.

For if that first covenant had been faultless, then should no place have been sought for the second.

For finding fault with them, he saith, Behold, the days come, saith the Lord, when I will make a new covenant with the house of Israel and with the house of Judah:

Not according to the covenant that I made with their fathers in the day when I took them by the hand to lead them out of the land of Egypt; because they continued not in my covenant, and I regarded them not, saith the Lord.

For this is the covenant that I will make with the house of Israel after those days, saith the Lord; I will put my laws into their mind, and write them in their hearts: and I will be to them a God, and they shall be to me a people:

And they shall not teach every man his neighbor, and every man his brother, saying, Know the Lord: for all shall know me, from the least to the greatest.

For I will be merciful to their unrighteousness, and their sins and their iniquities will I remember no more.

In that he saith, A new covenant, he hath made the first old. <u>Now that which decayeth and waxeth old is ready to vanish away.</u>

[That is why it is called the Old Covenant!]

Hebrews 7:11-12

If therefore perfection were by the Levitical priesthood, (for under it the people received the law,) what further need was there that another priest should rise after the order of Melchisedec, and not be called after the order of Aaron?

For the priesthood being changed, there is made of necessity a change also of the law.

Hebrews 7:18

…For there is verily <u>a disannulling of the commandment</u> going before for the weakness and unprofitableness thereof.

[The Law is changed, it is disannulled, it is vanished away, it is old ... it is gone.]

Hebrews 9: 7-10

But into the second went the high priest alone once every year, not without blood, which he offered for himself, and for the errors of the people:

The Holy Ghost this signifying, that the way into the holiest of all was not yet made manifest, while as the first tabernacle was yet standing:

Which was a figure for the time then present, in which were offered both gifts and sacrifices, that could not make him that did the service perfect, as pertaining to the conscience;

Which stood only in meats and drinks, and divers washings, and carnal ordinances, imposed on them <u>until the time of reformation.</u>

[It was imposed until the reformation of the New Covenant. And now it is no longer imposed upon us.]

Hebrews 10:1

For the law having a shadow of good things to come, and not the very image of the things, can never with those sacrifices which they offered year by year continually make the comers thereunto perfect.

[If the sacrifices of the Old Covenant cannot make you perfect, then they cannot fully wash away sin. It must therefore be replaced with a covenant that can.]

Hebrews 10: 4

For it is not possible that the blood of bulls and of goats should take away sins.

[If the Old Testament sacrifices cannot take away sin, then it is of no value to us who are lost in sin because it cannot save us. There has to be a new covenant, or we are all lost.]

Hebrews 10: 8,9

Above when he said, Sacrifice and offering and burnt offerings and offering for sin thou wouldest not, neither hadst pleasure therein; which are offered by the law;

Then said he, Lo, I come to do thy will, O God. <u>He taketh away the first that he may establish the second.</u>

[He took away the first covenant. It is gone. He did that so He could usher us into a better covenant.]

Galatians 3:19

Wherefore then serveth the law? It was added because of transgressions, till the seed should come to whom the promise was made

[The purpose of the Old was to bring us to the New.]

Galatians 3: 24,25

Wherefore the law was our schoolmaster to bring us unto Christ, that we might be justified by faith. But after that faith is come, we are no longer under a schoolmaster.

Hebrews 13: 9,10

Be not carried about with divers and strange doctrines. For it is a good thing that the heart be established with grace; not with meats, which have not profited them that have been occupied therein.

We have an altar, whereof they (Levitical priests) have no right to eat which serve the tabernacle.

[If they stay with the doctrine of Mosaic law and refuse the Grace of Christ's blood, then they are excluded from the Altar of God from which we as Christians may partake.]

Ephesians 2:15

Having abolished in his flesh the enmity, <u>even the law of commandments</u> contained in ordinances; for to make in himself of twain one new man, so making peace;

[The Old Law was at enmity with us. The Old Covenant died when His physical body, the Word of God in the flesh, died on the Cross so that He, as the Word of God in the Spirit, would be able to rise from the dead for us.]

Colossians 2:14

Blotting out the handwriting of ordinances *(of the Old Law)* that was against us, which was contrary to us, and took it out of the way, nailing it to his cross;

[Christ gave His life to set us free from the Law. He abolished it and nailed it to His Cross. Why would anyone want to go back to that after He paid such a high price to set us free from it?]

Romans 2:14

For when the Gentiles, which have not the law, do by nature the things contained in the law, these, having not the law, are a law unto themselves: Which shew the work of the law written in their hearts,

Galatians 2:16

Knowing that a man is not justified by the works of the law, but by the faith of Jesus Christ, even we have believed in Jesus Christ, that we might be justified by the faith of Christ, and not by the works of the law: for by the works of the law shall no flesh be justified.

Romans 3:19-20

Now we know that what things soever the law saith, it saith to them who are under the law: *(not to those under Grace)* that every mouth may be stopped, and all the world may become guilty before God.

Therefore by the deeds of the law there shall no flesh be justified in his sight: for by the law is the knowledge of sin.

[You cannot be justified by the Law no matter how righteous you may be. The Law served to show us our sin.]

Romans 3: 21-22

But now the righteousness of God without the law is manifested, being witnessed by the law and the prophets;

Even the righteousness of God which is by faith of Jesus Christ unto all and upon all them that believe:

[The Law brought condemnation; the New Covenant brought Grace.]

Romans 5:20

Moreover the law entered, that the offence might abound. But where sin abounded, grace did much more abound:

Romans 11:6

And if by grace, then is it no more of works: otherwise grace is no more grace. But if it be of works, then is it no more grace: otherwise work is no more work.

Romans 3:28

Therefore we conclude that a man is justified by faith without the deeds of the law.

Philippians 3:9

And be found in him, not having mine own righteousness, which is of the law, but that which is through the faith of Christ, the righteousness which is of God by faith:

Romans 4:13-16

For the promise, that he should be the heir of the world, was not to Abraham, or to his seed, through the law, but through the righteousness of faith.

For if they which are of the law be heirs, faith is made void, and the promise made of none effect:

Because the law worketh wrath: for where no law is, there is no transgression.

Therefore it is of faith, that it might be by grace; to the end the promise might be sure to all the seed; not to that only which is of the law, but to that also which is of the faith of Abraham; who is the father of us all,

[You cannot have it both ways.]

Romans 6:14

For sin shall not have dominion over you: for ye are not under the law, but under grace.

[The wonderful thing about Grace is that it is not just a covering for sin, but it is the actual power that God gives you to overcome sin. That is what is different about Grace.]

Romans 7:1-5

Know ye not, brethren, (for I speak to them that know the law,) how that the law hath dominion over a man as long as he liveth?

For the woman which hath an husband is bound by the law to her husband so long as he liveth; but if the husband be dead, she is loosed from the law of her husband.

So then if, while her husband liveth, she be married to another man, she shall be called an adulteress: but if her husband be dead, she is free from that law; so that she is no adulteress, though she be married to another man.

Wherefore, my brethren, <u>ye also are become dead to the law by the body of Christ</u>; that ye should be married to another, even to him who is raised from the dead, that we should bring forth fruit unto God.

[We were delivered from the Old Law so that we could bring forth fruit. Fruit cannot grow on a dead tree.]

Romans 7:6

But now we are delivered from the law, that being dead wherein we were held; that we should serve in newness of spirit, and not in the oldness of the letter.

[We have been delivered! We were dead, but now we are alive.]

Romans 8:2-8

For the law of the Spirit of life in Christ Jesus hath made me free from the law of sin and death.

For what the law could not do, in that it was weak through the flesh, God sending his own Son in the likeness of sinful flesh, and for sin, condemned sin in the flesh:

That the righteousness of the law might be fulfilled in us, who walk not after the flesh, but after the Spirit.

For they that are after the flesh do mind the things of the flesh; but they that are after the Spirit the things of the Spirit.

<u>For to be carnally minded is death</u>; but to be spiritually minded is life and peace.

Because the carnal mind is enmity against God: for it is not subject to the law of God, neither indeed can be.

So then they that are in the flesh cannot please God.

[If you follow the Law of sin and death, you cannot please God. How then would you think that it will usher you into Heaven?]

Romans 9:30-32

What shall we say then? That the Gentiles, which followed not after righteousness, have attained to righteousness, even the righteousness which is of faith.

But Israel, which followed after the law of righteousness, hath not attained to the law of righteousness.

Wherefore? Because they sought it not by faith, but as it were by the works of the law. For they stumbled at that stumbling stone;

Romans 10:4

For Christ is the end of the law for righteousness to everyone that believeth.

Ephesians 2:14-16

For he is our peace, who hath made both one, and hath broken down the middle wall of partition between us;

Having abolished in his flesh the enmity, even the law of commandments contained in ordinances; for to make in himself of twain one new man, so making peace;

And that he might reconcile both unto God in one body by the cross, having slain the enmity thereby:

Philippians. 3:2-9

Beware of dogs, beware of evil workers, beware of the concision. For we are the circumcision, which worship God in the spirit, and rejoice in Christ Jesus, and have no confidence in the flesh.

[The Concision comes from a word in the Greek that means "meat butchers". By using this word, Paul is making a sarcastic comment about those who demand circumcision. The true circumcision is the one in the Spirit that is a circumcision of the heart.]

2Corinthians 3:7

But if the ministration of death, written and engraven in stones, was glorious, so that the children of Israel could not stedfastly behold the face of Moses for the glory of his countenance; <u>which glory was to be done away:</u>

2 Corinthians 3:13-15

And not as Moses, which put a vail over his face, that the children of Israel could not stedfastly look to the end of that which is abolished:

But their minds were blinded: for until this day remaineth the same vail untaken away in the reading of the old testament; which vail is done away in Christ.

But even unto this day, when Moses is read, the vail is upon their heart.

Psalms 108:8

Gilead is mine; Manasseh is mine; Ephraim also is the strength of mine head; Judah is my lawgiver;

[Judah, not Moses. If the Levitical Law was to be the Lawgiver, David would have said Levi or Moses. Jesus, the lawgiver of the New Testament, came out of Judah.]

Galatians 2:20-21

I am crucified with Christ: nevertheless I live; yet not I, but Christ liveth in me: and the life which I now live in the flesh I live by the faith of the Son of God, who loved me, and gave himself for me.

I do not frustrate the grace of God: <u>for if righteousness come by the law, then Christ is dead in vain.</u>

Galatians 3:2-3

This only would I learn of you, Received ye the Spirit by the works of the law, or by the hearing of faith?

Are ye so foolish? <u>having begun in the Spirit, are ye now made perfect by the flesh?</u>

Galatians 3:10

For as many as are of the works of the law are under the curse: for it is written, Cursed is every one that continueth not in all things which are written in the book of the law to do them.

Galatians 3:11-13

But that no man is justified by the law in the sight of God, it is evident: for, The just shall live by faith.

And the law is not of faith: but, The man that doeth them shall live in them.

Christ hath redeemed us from the curse of the law, being made a curse for us: for it is written, Cursed is every one that hangeth on a tree:

[Christ took the curse of the Law to His grave. It died with Him, so that when He rose from the dead, He had conquered it and set us free.]

Galatians 4:21-25

Tell me, ye that desire to be under the law, do ye not hear the law?

For it is written, that Abraham had two sons, the one by a bondmaid, the other by a freewoman.

But he who was of the bondwoman was born after the flesh; but he of the freewoman was by promise.

Which things are an allegory: for these are the two covenants; the one from the mount Sinai, which gendereth to bondage, which is Agar.

For this Agar is mount Sinai in Arabia, and answereth to Jerusalem which now is, and is in bondage with her children.

Galatians 4:30-31

Nevertheless what saith the scripture?

Cast out the bondwoman and her son: for the son of the bondwoman shall not be heir with the son of the freewoman.

[The Old Covenant cannot exist side-by-side with the New because it nullifies the Blood of Jesus Christ. It must be cast out.]

Galatians 5:1-5

Stand fast therefore in the liberty wherewith Christ hath made us free, and <u>be not entangled again with the yoke of bondage</u>.

Behold, I Paul say unto you, that if ye be circumcised, Christ shall profit you nothing.

For I testify again to every man that is circumcised, that he is a debtor to do the whole law.

Christ is become of no effect unto you, whosoever of you are justified by the law; ye are fallen from grace.

For we through the Spirit wait for the hope of righteousness by faith.

Galatians 5:18

But if ye be led of the Spirit, ye are not under the law.

*And the veil of the temple
was rent in twain
from the top to the bottom.*

Mark 15:38

About the Author

Dalen Garris has been in ministry since the Jesus Movement in California in 1970. In 1997, he began a radio broadcast that ultimately spread to dozens of countries, from Israel and Saudi Arabia to Africa and the Philippines. His program, *Fire in the Hole*, was broadcast for several years across North America on the Sky Angel network as the Voice of Jerusalem.

A newspaper column followed, for which he has written over 700 articles, which have been published in local newspapers and Christian magazines in several countries. He has also written over a dozen books and several booklets.

Since 2004, he has been lighting the fires of revival in churches spread across sub-Saharan Africa. Over the course of 17 years, he has preached in over 1,000 churches and has seen hundreds of them set on fire and explode in revival with hundreds of new ones planted across Africa.

And the fires are still burning.

Because of his work across Africa, Dalen Garris was awarded an honorary Doctorate in 2017 by the Northwestern Christian University of Florida.

Dr. Garris currently lives with Cindy, his wife of 44 years, in Waxahachie and is still heavily involved with churches across Africa. His pressing hope is in seeing this powerful move of God in Africa ignite us here in America. He believes that this upcoming generation will be the Gideon Generation that will usher in this last, great revival.

If you would like Dr. Garris to speak at your church or organization, please contact us for times and schedules.

Publications

Books:

Four Steps to Revival
Fire in the Hole
The Kenya Diaries
A Trumpet in Nigeria
A Scent of Rain
Into the Heart of Darkness
Fire and Rain
Do You Have Eternal Security?
Standing in the Gap – True and False Prophets
Revival Campaigns in Africa - 2019
A Voice in the Wilderness Series:
- vol. 1, Journey Begins
- vol. 2, The Early Years
- vol. 3, Prophet Rising
- vol. 4, Revival in the Wings
- vol. 5, The Sound of Abundance of Rain
- vol. 6, Watchman, What of the Night?
- vol. 7, Mud and Heroes

- Available at: **www.Revivalfire.org/books/**

Booklets:

A Volcano in Cape Verde
Tanzania, 2011
Nigeria, 2012
Planting a Seed in Liberia
A Whisper in the Wind
Finishing What We Started
Calvinism Critiqued
10 Days in Nairobi
A Light in the Bush

- Available for free at:
www.Revivalfire.org/booklets/

RevivalFire Ministries

PO Box 822
Waxahachie, TX 75168
dale@revivalfire.org

http://RevivalFire.org

www.ingramcontent.com/pod-product-compliance
Lightning Source LLC
Chambersburg PA
CBHW070858050426
42453CB00012B/2268